NEWPORT PUBLIC LIBRARY

3 1540 00293 0   S0-BHR-998

j608.03 Sto
Stoyles, Pennie
The A to Z of inventions
and inventors
31540002930699
v. 4

DISCARD

Newport Public Library

SEP 2 8 2009

Pennie Stoyles and Peter Pentland

The A to Z of
Inventions
and Inventors

Volume 4: M to P

Smart Apple Media

3 1540 00293 0699

This edition first published in 2006 in the United States of America by Smart Apple Media.
Reprinted 2007 (twice)

All rights reserved. No part of this book may be reproduced in any form or by any means without written permission from the Publisher.

Smart Apple Media
2140 Howard Drive West
North Mankato
Minnesota 56003

First published in 2006 by
MACMILLAN EDUCATION AUSTRALIA PTY LTD
15-19 Claremont Street, South Yarra, Australia 3141

Visit our website at www.macmillan.com.au

Associated companies and representatives throughout the world.

Copyright © Pennie Stoyles and Peter Pentland 2006

Library of Congress Cataloging-in-Publication Data

Stoyles, Pennie.
  The A to Z of inventions and inventors / Pennie Stoyles and Peter Pentland.
  p. cm.
  Contents: v. 1 A to B – v. 2. C to F – v. 3. G to L – v. 4. M to P – v. 5. Q-S – v.6 T-Z.
  ISBN-13: 978-1-58340-804-9 (v. 1)
  ISBN-13: 978-1-58340-805-6 (v. 2)
  ISBN-13: 978-1-58340-788-2 (v. 3)
  ISBN-13: 978-1-58340-789-9 (v. 4)
  ISBN-13: 978-1-58340-790-5 (v. 5)
  ISBN-13: 978-1-58340-791-2 (v. 6)
  1. Inventions—History—20th century—Encyclopedias. 2. Inventors—Biography—Encyclopedias.
  I. Pentland, Peter. II. Title.
  T20.S76 2006
  608.03—dc22   2005057602

Edited by Sam Munday
Text and cover design by Ivan Finnegan, iF design
Page layout by Ivan Finnegan, iF design
Photo research by Legend Images
Illustrations by Alan Laver, Shelly Communications

Printed in USA

Acknowledgments
The author and the publisher are grateful to the following for permission to reproduce copyright material:

Front cover: photo of matches courtesy of Photolibrary/Adrienne Hart-Davis/Science Photo Library.

Photos courtesy of:
3M, p. 30; Australian Picture Library/Corbis, p. 28; Corbis Digital Stock, p. 5; Digital Vision, p. 19; Dreamstime, p. 20; Getty Images, p. 31 (left); Legendimages, pp. 6, 22 (top right); Photodisc, p. 22 (top left and bottom); Photolibrary/Kraig Carlstrom, p. 25; Photolibrary/Foodpix, p. 24; Photolibrary/ Index Stock Imagery, p. 14; Photolibrary/Mauritius Die Bildagentur Gmbh, p. 31 (right); Photolibrary/ Photonica, p. 16; Photolibrary/CC Studio/Science Photo Library, p. 4; Photolibrary/Adrienne Hart-Davis/Science Photo Library, p. 7; Photolibrary/Workbook, Inc., p. 17; Photoobjects, © 2005 JupiterImages Corporation, p. 29; Photos.com, pp. 18 (all), 26; Raytheon Company, p. 10 (left); NMPFT/ Science & Society Picture Library, p. 12; Science Museum/Science & Society Picture Library, p. 8; Whirlpool, p. 10 (right).

While every care has been taken to trace and acknowledge copyright, the publisher tenders their apologies for any accidental infringement where copyright has proved untraceable. Where the attempt has been unsuccessful, the publisher welcomes information that would redress the situation.

Inventions

Welcome to the exciting world of inventions.

The A to Z of Inventions and Inventors is about inventions that people use every day. Sometimes these inventions happen by accident. Sometimes they come from a moment of inspiration. Often they are developed from previous inventions. In some cases, inventors race against each other to invent a machine.

Volume 4: M to P inventions

They said it!

"If I had thought about it, I wouldn't have done the experiment. The literature was full of examples that said you can't do this."

Spencer Silver on the work that led to the unique glues for Post-it® Notes.

Margarine

Margarine is a processed food that is used instead of butter.

Who invented margarine?

Margarine was invented by a French chemist called Hippolyte Mège-Mouriès in 1869.

The margarine story

In Europe during the 1800s, people were moving from farms (where they made their own butter), to cities (where they had to buy butter). Butter was becoming very expensive and hard to find. Refrigerators had not yet been invented so the butter spoiled easily. Hippolyte Mège-Mouriès was asked by the French Emperor, Louis Napoleon III, to make a substitute for butter. He churned ox fat and cream together to make margarine. This early margarine was colored white.

Many people use margarine instead of butter.

Margarine timeline

1869	1917	1952	1956	1966
Margarine was made from ox fat and cream	Coconut oil was used instead of ox fat to make margarine	The first soft margarine in a tub was made	The first spread made of butter and margarine was made	Low-fat margarine was invented

How margarine works

Margarine contains about 80 percent fat or oil. The rest is made up of water, colorings, flavorings, vitamins, and sometimes salt. The fat in most margarine comes from plants, such as canola, peanuts, and sunflower seeds. These plant fats contain less cholesterol than butter. Cholesterol is one of the causes of high blood pressure. Many people eat margarine instead of butter because they believe it is healthier.

Margarine is made from vegetable oil taken from plants such as sunflowers.

Changes to margarine over time

Some margarine contains a substance from plants called sterol. Sterol can help to lower the cholesterol levels in your blood. People with high blood pressure caused by cholesterol can use this type of margarine to lower their blood pressure.

Related invention

Butter has been around for so long that nobody knows who invented it. The ancient Greeks used it to treat burns and the ancient Romans smeared it in their hair as a beauty product.

A match is a thin piece of wood coated at one end with a chemical. When the coated end, called the head, is rubbed against a rough surface, it catches fire.

Who invented the match?

John Walker, an English pharmacist, invented the match in 1827.

The match story

Before the invention of matches, people would start fires by striking a piece of hard rock called flint with a piece of steel. This would produce a spark which could be used to start a fire.

John Walker's match had a mix of chemicals in its head. It would catch fire when rubbed against paper coated with ground glass.

In 1830 a Frenchman, Charles Sauria, adapted Walker's match by putting white phosphorus in the head. The match worked better, but it was dangerous.

Friction between the match and the side of the box makes it catch fire.

Did you know?

White phosphorus attacks the bones, especially in the jaw. Thousands of people working in match factories were killed or maimed because of white phosphorus poisoning. White phosphorus was replaced in matches in 1911.

How matches work

Matches have part of the burning material on the head and part on the side of the box. This reduces the chance that the matches will accidentally catch fire.

The head of a match contains the chemical potassium chlorate. Red phosphorus is glued to the side of the box. When they are rubbed together, the friction creates heat and starts a chemical reaction between the substances. This sets fire to the wood.

Safety matches do not explode in your pocket.

Changes to matches over time

You can now buy matches that are waterproof. These are useful when camping or taking part in water activities, like canoeing.

Related invention

In 1928, Louis Aronson invented a lighter that was fueled by gas. Once it was lit, it would stay alight until the gas supply to the flame was stopped.

Microphone

A microphone converts sound into electricity. It allows us to record sounds, make them louder, or transmit them over large distances using radio or telephones.

Who invented the microphone?

The first microphone was invented by English-born music professor David Hughes in 1878.

The microphone story

In 1876, Emile Berliner invented the first simple microphone to improve the quality of the telephone.

David Hughes also tried to improve the quality of sound of the telephone. One of his first microphones had two nails lying side-by-side with a third nail lying across them. It was so sensitive that it could detect a fly walking near it, but it was not useful for telephones. In 1878, Hughes improved his design for the microphone by putting carbon grains between two metal plates.

David Hughes invented the three-nail microphone in 1878.

Microphone timeline

1827	1876	1878	1942	1962
Sir Charles Wheatstone invents the word microphone	Emile Berliner invents the first microphone as a way of improving Bell's telephone	David Hughes invents the carbon microphone	The ribbon microphone is invented for use in radio broadcasting	Bell Laboratories invent the electret microphone

How the microphone works

The microphone works by changing sound waves into electrical signals in order to amplify them. When a person speaks into a microphone, sound waves hit a thin sheet of metal called a diaphragm and make it vibrate. When the diaphragm vibrates, a voice coil vibrate next to a magnet also vibrates, creating electric signals. The electric signals travel along a wire to the amplifier and speakers, so the sound can be heard at a louder volume.

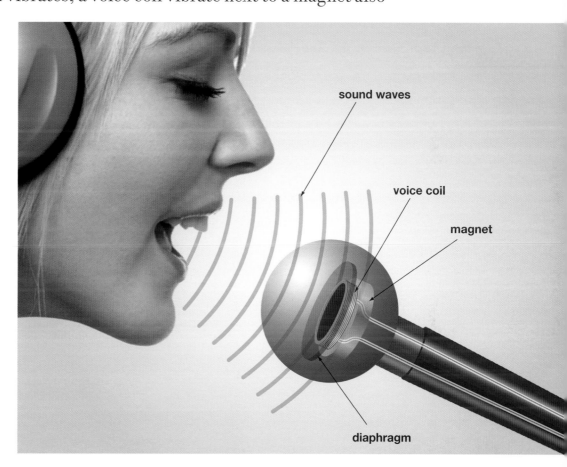

sound waves

voice coil

magnet

diaphragm

Changes to microphones over time

Sound engineers have been constantly improving the quality of microphones so that the electric signal they produce is a very accurate for all sorts of sounds.

Related inventions

The telephone was invented by Alexander Graham Bell in 1876.
The radio was invented by Guglielmo Marconi in 1896.

Microwave oven

A microwave oven is a machine that uses **microwaves**, rather than heat from electricity or fuel, to cook food.

Who invented the microwave oven?

Percy Spencer, an American engineer, invented the microwave oven in 1947.

The microwave oven story

The magnetron is an electronic device that makes microwaves. It was invented during World War II to help detect enemy airplanes attacking Britain.

After the war, Percy Spencer was experimenting with a magnetron when he noticed that a chocolate bar in his pocket had melted. He thought the microwaves had caused this to happen. He experimented with other foods such as popcorn and an egg. Spencer's assistant was looking closely at the egg when it exploded in his face. Spencer went on to design and **patent** the microwave oven.

Percy Spencer invented the microwave oven in 1947.

Microwave ovens can quickly cook or heat food.

Did you know?

The first microwave oven was over 5 feet (1.5 m) tall and weighed 772 pounds (350 kg). It cost $5,000, more than twice the amount of money the average worker earned in a year.

How microwave ovens work

The main part of a microwave oven is the magnetron. It makes microwaves. The microwaves travel along a pipe and hit a rotating paddle. This spreads the microwaves evenly around the oven.

The food is placed on a rotating dish. The microwaves travel easily through the food. They stimulate water molecules in the food, making them hot. The heat flows from the water to the rest of the food and warms it. Microwave ovens can heat or cook food much more quickly than normal gas and electric ovens.

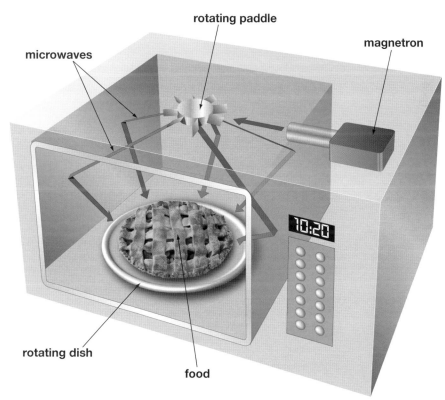

rotating paddle

magnetron

microwaves

10:20

rotating dish

food

Changes to microwave ovens over time

Microwave ovens are now much smaller and lighter than Spencer's original model. They can be programmed to start at certain times.

Related invention

The electric oven was invented in 1891 by the Carpenter Electric Heating Manufacturing Company.

Glossary words

microwaves types of electromagnetic radiation, such as light
patent a right granted to make, use, or sell something which is new, inventive, and useful

Moving pictures, or "movies," are a series of still pictures that are shown very quickly on a screen.

Who invented moving pictures?

William Dickson invented moving pictures in the United States in 1893.

The moving pictures story

Thomas Edison invented the record player in 1877. He thought that people would get bored listening to it if they did not have something to look at as well. He set his assistant William Dickson the task of solving the problem. In 1893, Dickson invented a moving picture camera called the kinematograph. This camera took forty pictures per second. People paid money to see the developed film in machines called "kinetoscopes."

In 1895, French brothers, Auguste and Louis Lumière, invented the **Cinematographe**. They made movies and were the first to show them to audiences in a theatre.

This kinetoscope was used to view moving pictures before film projectors were invented.

Moving pictures timeline

1893	1895	1909
Dickson invented the movie camera	Lumière brothers showed movies on a screen in a theatre	American Windsor McKay made the first animated movie, *Gertie the Dinosaur*

How moving pictures work

A movie camera winds a long strip of film from one reel to another. The film is briefly stopped and a shutter opens, forming a still image on the film. It is a similar process to how a camera works, only this happens 24 times per second in movie cameras.

The film is developed and **edited** to make a finished product, such as a story. A projector briefly stops the film and the shutter opens to show each still picture on the screen. This also happens 24 times per second. We see smooth movement because the eye retains each picture for a fraction of a second.

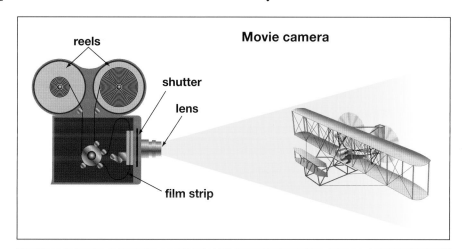

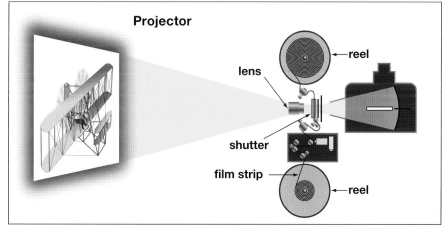

A movie camera and a projector.

Changes to moving pictures over time

Movies can now be shown on giant screens and in three dimensions. They use surround sound, with loudspeakers located all around the theater.

Related invention

Television was invented in 1923. It later allowed people to view movies in their own homes.

Glossary words

Cinematographe	a camera that could also be used to show movies
edited	cut and arranged in the correct order

Neon lights have tubes that contain neon gas. They give off a bright orange-red color when the gas is **excited** by electricity.

Who invented neon lights?

French scientist, Georges Claude, invented neon lights in 1910.

The neon lights story

In 1910 a French scientist, Georges Claude, found that a tube of neon gas gave off a bright orange-red color when he ran an electric current through it. He displayed two 115-feet (35-m) long neon tubes at the Paris Motor Show that year. An advertising agency thought they could use neon lights for signs. The first neon sign was used over the door of a Montmartre barber shop in 1912.

Neon lights timeline

1910	1912	1930s	1946
Georges Claude discovered that excited neon gas gives off light	The first neon sign was put up over a barber shop in Montmartre	Neon lights were used in Times Square in New York and Piccadilly Circus in London	Neon lights were used in Las Vegas

Neon lights can look very impressive.

How neon lights work

When electricity passes through the neon gas, it gives energy to the **atoms**. The atoms use this energy by giving off light.

If other chemicals are added to neon tubes they make them give off other colors. Mercury vapor added to neon gas turns the light blue or green.

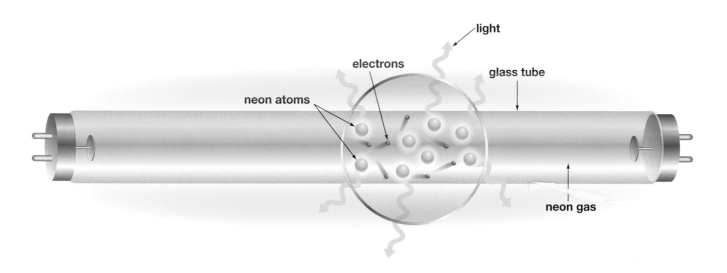

Electricity excites neon gas to make it give off light.

Changes to neon lights over time

Neon lights are now used all over the world, especially for advertising signs. Small neon lights are now used to decorate household items such as telephones. Neon lights are also used in making works of art.

Related invention

Edmund Germer invented fluorescent tubes in 1927. They contain mercury vapor but work in a similar way to neon lights.

Glossary words

excited	charged with energy
atoms	incredibly tiny particles that combine to make up everything in the world

Non-stick pan

Non-stick pans are saucepans and frying pans that are coated with a special plastic called Teflon®.

Who invented the non-stick pan?

The non-stick pan was invented by Marc Gregoire, in 1954 in France.

The non-stick pan story

In 1938 an American scientist, Dr. Roy Plunkett, accidentally discovered Teflon®. He was experimenting with different gases and left one batch overnight in a container. When he arrived the next day, the container was filled with a very slippery solid which could not be changed by chemicals. This solid was tetrafluoroethylene, which Dr. Plunkett called Teflon®.

In the early 1950s, a Frenchman, Marc Gregoire, learned of Teflon® and put it on his fishing tackle to stop it tangling. His wife came up with the idea of putting it on pots and pans. Gregoire coated one of her frying pans with great success. In a few years, he was selling more than a million non-stick pans a year.

Did you know?

The *Guinness World Records* lists Teflon® as the slipperiest substance on Earth.

An egg easily slips off a non-stick pan.

How non-stick pans work

The coating on non-stick pans is much more slippery than the metal underneath. If you looked at the surface of a metal pan under a strong microscope, you would see small grooves and holes which the food sticks to. A coating of Teflon® fills in all the grooves and holes, making a smooth and slippery surface so there is no way for the food to stick to the pan.

Teflon® coating is sprayed on so that it covers the surface evenly.

Changes to non-stick pans over time

Since the invention of Teflon®, new non-stick coatings have been invented. One is a mixture of titanium metal with **ceramics** that is sandblasted onto the pan. It is then fired to 36,032°F (20,000°C) and coated with a non-stick material. These pans last a lifetime, but they are very expensive.

Related invention

Teflon® is used to keep clothing and carpets looking newer for longer. It is also used to make space suits.

Glossary word

ceramics   materials such as china that have to be fired in a kiln

17

Nylon

Nylon is a synthetic, artificial fiber that belongs to a group of substances called polymers.

Who invented nylon?

Nylon was invented by a chemist, Wallace Carothers, in 1935 in the U.S.

The nylon story

In the late 1920s, chemical companies were researching ways to make new products. Wallace Carothers was working on new, synthetic fibers that could be used to make fabrics. In 1935 he discovered how to make a fiber with the chemical name of polyhexamethyleneadiapamide, or "polymer 66." After two more years of research, it was patented and renamed nylon. The first nylon fibers were used for fishing line and toothbrush bristles. By 1940, nylon was being used instead of silk for women's stockings. During World War II it was also used instead of silk to make parachutes.

All of these things are made from nylon.

Did you know?
In the U.S., the word "nylons" means stockings.

How nylon works

Nylon is made from chemicals that come from coal, oil, and natural gas. Nylon fibers are made by heating up the nylon until it is a liquid, then forcing it through small holes. The liquid then cools into long stretchy fibers. Nylon fibers are tough and waterproof and they can withstand temperatures up to 500°F (260°C). Nylon fabric does not absorb water, so it dries very quickly.

The toughness of nylon makes it an ideal material for a spacesuit.

Changes to nylon over time

Nylon is used in making the Apollo space suits. The inside layer of the space suit is made of nylon. Other layers are also made of nylon as well as neoprene and Teflon®.

Related invention

Wallace Carothers' other famous invention is neoprene, which is a synthetic rubber. Neoprene is used to make many things including wetsuits, car fanbelts, and knee braces.

Outboard motor

An outboard motor is a motor that is attached to the back of a small boat. It is used to propel a boat through water at fast speeds.

Who invented the outboard motor?

The outboard motor was invented by Ole Evinrude in 1907.

The outboard motor story

Ole Evinrude was born in Norway in 1877. His family moved to America five years later. On a hot day in 1906, Ole had to row a boat for five miles to get ice cream for his fiancé. This inspired him to think up a way of attaching a small motor to the back of the boat.

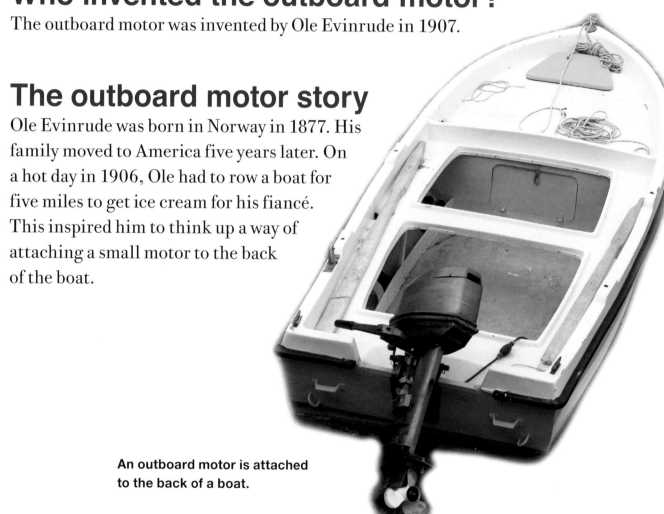

An outboard motor is attached to the back of a boat.

Outboard motor timeline

1907	1911	1914	1919	1929
Evinrude builds and tests his first outboard motor	Evinrude goes into business with a tugboat company owner	Evinrude sells his half of the business so he and his wife can take a vacation	Evinrude designs and builds a lighter, stronger motor and sets up another company	Evinrude buys back his original company

How outboard motors work

An outboard motor has a long shaft that connects the engine to a propeller. The engine makes the shaft spin. The shaft is connected to a propeller by gears that change the direction of the spinning from vertical to horizontal.

When the propeller spins, the blades push water away from the boat. The water pushes against the propeller blades which makes the boat move forward. The engine speed is controlled by twisting a lever called the throttle. The outboard motor is very similar to that of a lawnmower engine.

throttle

engine

shaft

gears

propeller

Changes to outboard motors over time

Early outboard motors were hand-made, had a water-cooling system, were quite heavy and used a two cycle system to burn fuel for power. Modern outboard motors are mass produced. Many use a four cycle system like a car engine to burn the fuel. The engines are cooled by air. They are quieter, more powerful, and cause less pollution to our waterways.

Related inventions

The Victa motor mower was invented in 1952 by Mervyn Victor Richardson. It was the first lawn mower to have blades attached to a horizontally spinning disc.

Paper is a material made from wood pulp.

Who invented paper?

The process we use for making paper today was invented by a Chinese man, called Ts'ai Lun, in 105 BCE.

The paper story

Over 5,000 years ago, before the invention of paper, the ancient Egyptians made papyrus to write on. They pressed thin layers of papyrus pith together and dried them in the sun.

Modern paper is made by grinding up wood or other plant material into a pulp before making it into thin sheets. This process was invented by Ts'ai Lun, over 2,000 years ago. He used scraps of silk and the bark from mulberry trees to make his paper.

All these things are made from paper.

Paper timeline

Early 1600s	1798	1806	1900
The first newspapers were printed	The first paper-making machine was invented in France	Carbon paper was invented	The paperclip was patented by a Norwegian man called John Vaaler

How paper works

Paper is usually made from wood which is chipped into small pieces. It is then made into a mushy pulp by cooling it with water and other chemicals. The pulp is sprayed onto a fine screen. Gradually, a thin layer of wood fibers collects on the screen and the water drains away. The layer of wood fibers is squeezed, rolled flat, and dried until the pulp turns into paper.

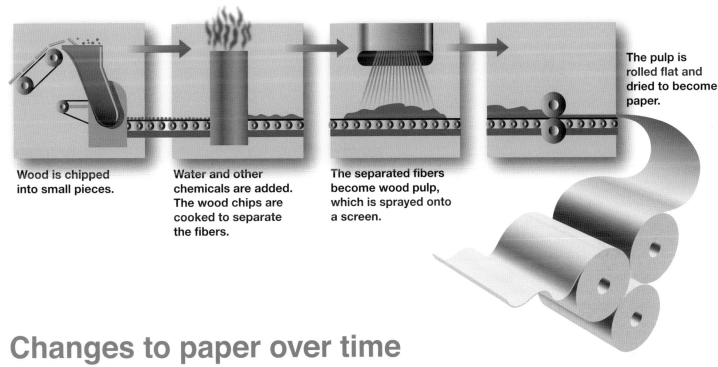

Wood is chipped into small pieces.

Water and other chemicals are added. The wood chips are cooked to separate the fibers.

The separated fibers become wood pulp, which is sprayed onto a screen.

The pulp is rolled flat and dried to become paper.

Changes to paper over time

Electronic reusable paper is being developed. It is like a thin sheet of plastic which contains millions of tiny beads. The beads are black on one side and white on the other. By using a special wand, the page will display words or pictures by rotating the beads–with the black side up to show print.

Related invention

The paper plate was the first "throw-away" food service product. It was invented in 1904. Paper cups were invented in 1908.

Pasteurization

Pasteurization is a process that helps to preserve foods such as milk and fruit juices.

Who invented pasteurization?

Frenchman Nicholas Appert discovered the process that would become known as pasteurization.

The pasteurization story

In 1795, Nicholas Appert found that by gently heating and then cooling milk, it would stay fresh much longer, but he did not know why. Fifty years later, a French chemist, called Louis Pasteur, discovered many things about microscopic organisms called bacteria. He discovered that bacteria caused foods to go bad and he proved that heating killed many of the bacteria. The word "pasteurization" was given to the heating process in his honor.

Milk and fruit juice are pasteurized so they do not spoil so quickly.

Louis Pasteur (1822–1895)

Louis Pasteur studied sciences and mathematics and became a professor of physics. He researched many areas of science but is most famous for his research on microorganisms. In addition to discovering pasteurization, he discovered how microorganisms make beer and wine. He also developed **vaccines** for many infectious diseases.

How pasteurization works

Pasteurization works by killing some of the bacteria and destroying **enzymes** that cause food to spoil. Bacteria are all around us, in the air and on the surfaces we touch. Some foods naturally contain substances called enzymes that cause them to spoil.

Milk is pasteurized by heating it to 145°F (63°C) for 30 minutes or 164°F (73°C) for 15 seconds. If the milk was boiled, all the bacteria would be destroyed, but you would also change the taste of the milk. Pasteurized milk needs to be kept in the refrigerator.

Milk is pasteurized in factories before it is packaged for sale.

Changes to pasteurization over time

Ultra heat treated, or UHT, milk can be kept out of the refrigerator. In UHT pasteurization, the temperature of the milk is raised to about 286°F (141°C) for one or two seconds, killing all the bacteria in the milk. UHT milk tastes different from fresh milk.

Related inventions

Louis Pasteur also invented vaccines for three diseases: chicken cholera, anthrax, and rabies.

Glossary words

vaccines	medicines that prevent diseases
enzymes	natural chemicals found in most foods

Photocopier

A photocopier is a machine that uses light to create a copy of a document, drawing, or page.

Who invented the photocopier?

American office worker, Chester F. Carlson, invented the photocopier in 1938.

The photocopier story

Chester F. Carlson worked in a patent office. He often had to make copies of drawings and documents. He thought there had to be a quicker way to make copies than photographing them. He started to experiment and in 1938 invented a process called xerography, but he was not able to find anyone to develop it.

Ten years later, a small photo-paper manufacturer called Haloid decided to work on xerography. The company is now called Xerox. They made the first office photocopier in 1959.

Did you know?

In the early 1900s, photography was used to copy documents. This process was slow and expensive.

Photocopiers are used in libraries and offices to copy documents.

How photocopiers work

Photocopiers have five main parts, a window, a bright light source, a toner cartridge, a highly polished drum, and a fuser. The document is placed on the window. A bright light shines on it. The light is reflected onto the drum where **static electricity** attracts the toner to the drum. This is transferred to the copy paper and fused onto the page using heat. The copy is then carried out of the machine.

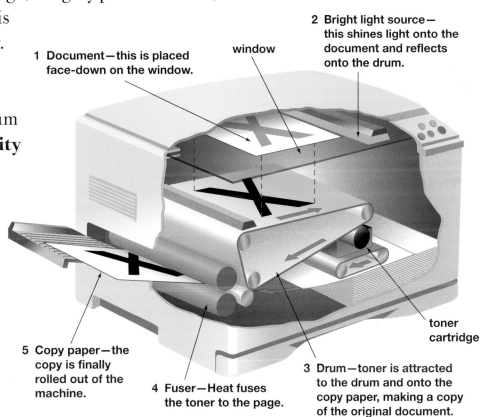

1 Document—this is placed face-down on the window.

window

2 Bright light source— this shines light onto the document and reflects onto the drum.

toner cartridge

5 Copy paper—the copy is finally rolled out of the machine.

4 Fuser—Heat fuses the toner to the page.

3 Drum—toner is attracted to the drum and onto the copy paper, making a copy of the original document.

Changes to photocopiers over time

Photocopiers have developed a great deal since they were first invented. They are now much faster, can copy on both sides of a piece of paper, sort pages into the right order, and staple them. Some models can copy in color.

Related invention

The flatbed computer scanner and its software was invented in 1974 by a team lead by Raymond Kurzweil. It was part of a computerized machine that could read books and documents for the blind.

Plastic

Plastic is a man-made substance used instead of glass, wood, metals, and other materials. There are many types of plastic.

Who invented plastic?

The first man-made plastic was called Bakelite. It was named after Leo Baekeland, who invented it in 1907 in America.

The plastic story

The very first plastics were called "man-modified" plastics. Naturally occurring substances, such as cellulose which is found in plants, were chemically treated to make new materials.

Bakelite was the first completely man-made plastic. Bakelite is a liquid that sets quickly to form a solid. It can be molded into any shape. Once it has set, it does not burn, melt, or dissolve. Hundreds of other plastics have been invented since Bakelite, and they have millions of different uses.

These clocks and radios are made from Bakelite.

Plastic timeline

1907	1913	1939	1946	1949	1973
Bakelite was invented	Cellophane was invented	Nylon stockings were first sold	Tupperware® was invented	Silly Putty® was invented	Plastic soda bottles were invented

How plastic works

Plastics are usually made from chemicals that are extracted from coal, oil, or natural gas. Plastics are sometimes called **polymers**. The word polymer means many parts. Plastics are made by chemically joining many smaller **molecules** called monomers. Plastics can also be made into thin fibers and woven into cloth. Some plastics can be made into thin sheets and used for plastic bags and cling wrap. Some plastics are flexible while others are really tough.

Plastics are used to make many different things, such as toys.

Changes to plastic over time

People today are concerned about what to do with waste plastic. Plastic does not rot as easily as paper, metal, or wood. Many plastic household items are now marked with a symbol which shows if it can be recycled. People have also invented many ways of using recycled plastic.

Related inventions

Earl Tupper invented plastic containers with air-tight lids called Tupperware. Tupperware did not sell well in stores because people did not know how to use the lids, so he invented a system of demonstrating and selling his product in people's homes called Tupperware Parties. It is estimated that every two seconds, a Tupperware party is starting somewhere in the world.

Glossary word

molecules	a group of atoms
polymer	molecules that are made by joining many smaller molecules together

Post-it® Notes

Post-it® Notes are small notes that have a strip of glue along one edge. The glue can be easily separated and reused many times.

Who invented Post-it® Notes?

Dr. Spencer Silver and Art Fry invented Post-it® Notes in the U.S. between 1968 and 1974.

The Post-it® Notes story

In 1968, Dr. Spencer Silver was trying to make very sticky glue for a company called 3M. He accidentally developed a semi-sticky glue instead. This glue could be re-used without leaving sticky bits behind when it was peeled off.

Meanwhile Art Fry, another worker at 3M, was singing in his church choir and worrying about how to stop the bookmarks slipping out of his hymn book. He used Dr. Silver's glue to produce sticky bookmarks that could be peeled off and used again. One year later, the 3M company started to make Post-it® Notes.

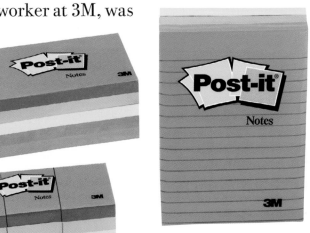

Post-it® Notes glue was invented by accident.

Did you know?

In 2002, an American artist called Vanalyne Green created a portrait of a cat called Juno using 50,000 Post-it® Notes. It measured 30 feet by 30 feet (9 m by 9 m).

How Post-it® Notes work

For glue to stick properly, it has to completely cover the surface you are sticking. Post-it® Note glue works because it doesn't cover the surface well. This glue is a called a **microsphere** adhesive. The tiny balls in the glue are separated with gaps between them. So, although each ball of glue is very sticky, the notes do not stick very strongly overall.

Post-it® Notes now come in many varieties and can be used for many purposes.

Changes to Post-it® Notes over time

An electronic version of Post-it® Notes is available for personal computers. Each note can fit about 32,000 characters. This is about as many characters as there are in this whole book!

Super Sticky Post-it® Notes are now available which can stick on virtually any surface. The Super Sticky Post-it® Notes use a new type of glue which is stronger than the one used on standard Post-it® Notes.

Related invention

In 1902, an Australian stationery company, Birchall's of Launceston, invented the first notepad.

Index

Page references in bold indicate that there is a full entry for that invention.